A short span of days

Meditation and care
for the dying patient, family and care-giver

Laurence Freeman, OSB

A short span of days

Meditation and care for the dying patient, family and care-giver

Talks given to
the Seventh International Congress
on Palliative Care

NOVALIS / MEDIO MEDIA / ARTHUR JAMES

A Short Span of Days is published by Novalis and Medio Media in association with Arther James Ltd. © 1996

Cover: direction, Jerome Herauf; design, Gilles Lépine
Layout: Gilles Lépine

Novalis Editorial Offices, Saint Paul University, 223 Main St.,
   Ottawa, Ontario, Canada K1S 1C4
Novalis Business Offices, 49 Front St. East, Second Floor
   Toronto, Ontario, Canada M5E 1B3
ISBN: 2-89088-865-7
Arthur James Ltd., 70 Cross Oak Road,
   Berkhamsted, Hertfordshire, England, HP4 3HZ
Medio Media
   23 Kensington Square, London, England, W8 5HN
ISBN: 0-85305-377-4
Printed in Canada.
Revised second edition. First published by Novalis in 1991.

Canadian Cataloguing in Publication Data

Freeman, Laurence
    A short span of days : meditation and care for
the dying patient, family and care-giver

Rev. 2nd ed.
Talks given to the seventh International Congress on
    Palliative Care, Montréal, Oct. 1988.
ISBN 2-89088-865-7

1. Church work with the terminally ill. 2. Church
work with the bereaved. 3. Terminal care–Religious
aspects–Christianity. 4. Meditation–Christianity.
I. International Congress on Palliative Care (7th : 1988
: Montréal, Quebec) II. Title.

BV4910.F74   1996   248.8'6   C96-900900-3

Contents

Foreword to the second edition · 7

Preface · 9

Meditation and the care of the terminally ill · 13

Keeping death before your eyes:
    Meditation and the dying person · 27

Being together in truth:
    Meditation and the family · 35

Companions toward death:
    Meditation and the care-giver · 45

Conclusion · 51

Foreword to the second edition

To some readers it may seem paradoxical that the setting for these reflections on meditation as a path toward richer, fuller living was a conference on care of the dying. In a series of presentations at the 1988 McGill International Congress on Care of the Terminally Ill, Father Laurence Freeman talked to nurses, doctors, social workers, psychologists, therapists of all disciplines and volunteers of all ages and walks of life – persons as varied as the cultures and countries they represented. *A Short Span of Days* is the transcript of those talks. They appear exactly as they occurred. In this unedited form they convey something of the freshness, simplicity and directness of the original encounters themselves.

Laurence reminds us that St. Benedict advised his monks to keep death constantly before their eyes. Why? What is to be gained through a continuing awareness of our transience? Those of us who have the dying as our daily teachers learn from them to value time, relationships and the potential in each moment. The world is seen through sharpened senses, the quest for meaning in a new light. As a colleague commented, "You know Bal, you can't do what we do for a living and still think that a Porsche will make it all better." We discover that we and those we care for are in fact in the same boat, accompanying one another, as we share the present moment and our quest for quality time.

Most of us are surprised to find that those who are approaching death through serious illness frequently experience quality time. How can it be that, in inching out of life, with what to us seemed many months of cruel suffering, the young world-class athlete commented, "This last year has been the best year of my life"? It seems remarkable that emotional well-being in one group of cancer patients was found to be the same as for the general population; amazing that life satisfaction does not necessarily decrease with progressive illness and has been found to be similar in cancer patients and persons who are completely healthy.

Even a sense of being "healthy" is completely compatible with terminal illness. For this feeling is dependent not on the presence or absence of disease, but on a sense of being able to "live fully," often in spite of physical infirmity. Indeed, some claim that they feel "healthier" since their diagnosis, due to changes in priorities, relationships, insight or mortality confronted. It is quite possible to die healed.

Quality of life, it turns out, is shaped, not by physical health, but by our experience of personal integrity, arising out of the web of our relationships with self, others, The Other, however conceived.

One evening at the Montreal Priory, John Main was asked by a new meditator, "Are you saying that meditation is the only path to inner peace?" Father John flashed his inimitable smile. "No," he replied. "But it's the only path I know." I would agree.

Balfour M. Mount, CM, OQ. MD, FRCS (C)
Eric M. Flanders Professor of Palliative Medicine
McGill University
Director, Palliative Care Service
Royal Victoria Hospital

Preface

Like meditation itself, this little book is practical in its aim. I hope that it will serve as an introduction to the experience of peace and depth – the depth where we find the source of life, particularly for those who have become conscious of their involvement with death. I say "conscious" because, of course, we are all involved with death. We die each day as we pass through all the phases of human development. We also die a little through the death of every other human being, even those we do not know. But generally we prefer to be unconscious of this involvement. Only when we are seriously ill ourselves, or someone we love is dying, or when we are caring for a dying person, do we become really conscious of death. And conscious of the vital role death plays in life.

Coming to this awareness can be difficult and painful. It is particularly painful if we have repressed or denied the reality of death before it becomes a fully personal event for us.

Meditation, like medicine, is an art concerned with care, attention and becoming whole through our woundedness. If we can learn to be still, silent and simple at the centre of our being, we grow in consciousness. We become more fully alive. And this is the aim of meditation. The light of consciousness is the light of God. It dispels the darkness of fear and the shadows of anger. We come to know that the light of consciousness is the light of life and that it enlightens everyone who is born into this world and who is reborn into the kingdom of God. In meditation we live the primal truth that we must die in order to be reborn.

We meditate as we are, where we are. In this sense is it ordinary. It is about taking ourselves as we are and accepting what is. For many people an experience of loss, of disruption or disappointment can lead to a breakdown of one sort or another. Breakdown is the opportunity for breakthrough into a life lived with a higher sense of reality. Meditation is about this breakthrough into reality and it can guide us through all the breakdowns of life as well as the ultimate breakdown we call death.

Birth and death are the most deeply personal events of life, but they are also communal. Our birth and death change the lives of others. The talks printed here concern the relationship between meditation and the event of death from the three perspectives of those concerned: the dying person, the family and friends of the dying person, and the professional care-giver. These three form a unity, a "therapeutic triad." The experience of meditation leads to an ever deeper and clearer awareness of how we are all related and inter-connected. The point of our unity is the spirit, the human dimension unrestricted by time and space. In the spirit we do not so much look at each other as objects or cases or problems. Instead we are conscious that we are deeply and redemptively involved with and for each other.

Healing happens as we move beyond objectification and into being-with. The healing of fear and anger, of loneliness and depression requires the energy of love. We channel this divine energy to each other through our neediness, our mortality, our poverty of spirit.

I hope that in their new format these talks can again help to recall these simple truths to people facing the ultimate poverty of the human condition, death itself. If meditation can lead us to the centre of our being where Truth dwells, then we naturally awaken in the light of the spirit to the power we have to communicate truthfully with each other in words of kindness and gestures of compassion.

Laurence Freeman, OSB
April 1991

Psalm 39

O Lord, you have shown me my end,
how short is the length of my days.
Now I know how fleeting is my life.
You have given me a short span of days;
my life is as nothing in your sight.
A mere breath, the one who stood so firm;
a mere shadow, the one who passes by;
a mere breath, the hoarded riches,
and who will take them, no one knows.
And now, Lord, what is there to wait for?
In you rests all my hope.
Set me free from the taunt of the fool.
I was silent, not opening my lips,
because this was all your doing.
Take away your scourge from me.
I am crushed by the blows of your hand.
You punish our sins and correct us;
like a moth you devour all we treasure.
Human life is no more than a breath;
O Lord, hear my prayer.
O Lord, turn your ear to my cry.
Do not be deaf to my tears.
In your house I am a passing guest,
a pilgrim, like all my forebears.
Look away that I may breathe again
before I depart to be no more.

Meditation and the care of the terminally ill

Let me begin at the end with these words, "And finally meditation is well-called in the tradition the 'first death.' It is the essential preparation for the second death which is our definitive entry into eternal life." It is especially significant for me to be here with you in this Congress. Six years ago I heard John Main conclude his talk with those words. It was his last major talk outside his monastery before his death. He was in pain as he spoke, and he was relieved after the talk when we drove back to the monastery to lay him down on his bed.

I'd like to tell you something of how he died because in his death he lived his teaching to the full. He lived life to the full. When he spoke about death he spoke about it with vitality. He didn't want to get off the train until he had gone as far as his ticket was meant to take him. But when he realized that death was coming up in the near future, he prepared himself fully for it. He threw himself into the process of dying with self-abandon; as fully as he committed himself to the process, the journey, of meditation; as fully as he was committed to God. His dying was a wondrous manifestation of the spiritual dimension of humankind. It was as if he was being filled with life to a point the body could not contain. He became powerfully silent. It was not the silence of being withdrawn from human contact, or regression of consciousness. It was the silence of an intensifying presence: the new person. When you were with him during that process of his dying you felt you were in the realm of spirit. You experienced the peace of his total centredness, the peace that is an energy, not just rest. There was joy, too, in his presence, a blissful certainty that human beings are the meaning of creation and that God is the meaning of the human being. There was also light, a spiritual light that gave an insight into reality deeper than words or thoughts. Invisible as that light was, you could see it. You could see it as Father John became increasingly translucent.

Now you could analyze the components of the peace that surrounded his death. You could say they were joy, certainty and light. But they were fused into one, each element was part of the other. Joy in the certainty and certainty of the light. I recognized it as the shalom that Christ breathed upon his disciples, as upon those who still had to go (as we still have to) through the second death. It was Christ's parting gift to the world; the peace that passes all understanding, all analysis.

Of course there were also tears. There was grief, there was pain and there was suffering. There must have been the human process of denial and anger and final acceptance. It was a perfectly human death, fully human. There was, early in the process, fear. Even Jesus feared his own death but he went through the wall of that fear. And he has left his disciples the peace to take them through it as well.

Peace is what makes death a human rather than a merely biological event. We seek peace because we are spiritual beings as well as beings that have a biological, mineral and chemical consciousness. We make peace because we seek peace. Happy the peacemakers, said Jesus, for they will inherit the earth. When we are at peace we are at one with our earth, our planet. We have found our place in creation. We are at home. If, as all the pious language says, death is a homecoming it must mean that it is a coming to a home within ourselves and within creation.

Now not everyone dies like Father John. Many seem to die still in the process of finding peace, indeed perhaps in the very early stages of finding it. They have not given themselves time in life to make peace. They often die in terrible fear because they have not gone through that wall of fear with its unresolved guilt, bitterness, anger or confusion. All that anguish is the death throes of the ego. Physical death, the second death, ends the ego for ever, and the ego does not go into the dark quietly. If the ego has not started to die before the second death begins, then death will be more anguished than it need be. Not everyone may have transcended their egoism as fully as John Main had when he came to die. But what John Main said and what he showed by the way he lived and died, and by the way he lived his death, is of great importance to us all. What he said six years ago I would repeat to you with the same conviction. "We must prepare for death. Just as we prepare for life by education, so we must prepare for death."

How can meditation empower you as care-givers to the dying to help people prepare for death? The best situation would be one in which meditation were part of our education from the beginning for all those in the therapeutic triad of patient, family and care-giver. If they had all been meditating for years, it would all be much easier. Peace would be that much closer. If meditation were as natural to them as eating, working, sleeping, making love, reading, making music, painting, going to school – if it were as natural as that, dying would be peaceful. But it seems to me that your work as care-givers to the terminally ill must logically lead you forward to the moment of death and back to the process of education. Not only to the end of the human life but to the beginning and the maturing of it. We are all terminally ill from birth. Somewhere in our DNA is the seed of mortality from conception. Because of that, the care-giver to the terminally ill must be led by the same essential values as the teacher, the priest or the humane administrator. People start to meditate at some particular point in their life, if they are graced to do so at all; but they start to meditate in much the same way that they fall in love. That is to say, quite unpredictably.

In our community we have taught children to meditate and we have shared meditation with patients at the Palliative Care Unit at the Royal Victoria Hospital. Age, personality-type, education or cultural background, none of those things make a person pre-disposed or unsuited for meditation. There is no measure of whether you are likely to make a good meditator or not. To say that someone is intrinsically unsuited to meditate is like saying that they are intrinsically incapable of love.

If meditation is a way to peace it is because it is a way to the centre of the human mystery, to the spirit, in which body and mind meet in a higher unity; in that third which all wholeness requires. If the therapeutic situation involves a triad of persons, then each of those persons is him or herself also a trinity of body, mind and spirit. Living that tri-unity fully is peace. Coming to it is wholeness.

In the Christian faith-vision of the human person the human being is an icon of God, a creature, but also a kind of hologram of God. Each of us reflects and contains the God who is three in one. Human wholeness is the wholeness, the holiness of God actively dwelling at the centre of our being. Now in meditation we accept the gift of our being in its wholeness. Silence is the context for that acceptance. In meditation we are not living from the mind or from the body alone but from the centre or what the tradition calls the heart. Meditation is not, therefore, concerned with what is particular to the mind: reasoning, imagining, judging, analyzing, verbalizing, picturing, conceptualizing. Meditation is deeper than words or thoughts; it is purely religious, that is spiritual, but it is not concerned with dogma. The only faith you need to begin to meditate is faith in the existence of your own centre. Neither is meditation concerned with what is particular to the body: movement, gesture, sensation, pain or pleasure.

Therefore the body is, ideally, perfectly still at the time of meditation; but we do not pretend that mental and bodily functions are suspended during meditation – distracting thoughts and an itchy nose! Meditation is concerned with that zone of unity we call the spirit, and the sign that we are in that zone is simplicity of consciousness. Simplicity is unity. God is simple. Each human being is fundamentally simple. We call it childlike. Meditation is simple; we enter that simplicity, and the peace that comes with it, by becoming silent and still.

Meditation is practical. It is not dogmatic or philosophical. It is experiential, not theoretical. There is a Zen story of two monks walking beside a river. The young monk is asking the older one all sorts of curious questions about the river: where has it come from, where is it going, how deep is it, how fast is it flowing, how cold is it. After a while the older monk loses his patience or seems to. He turns and pushes the young one into the river. As he helps him out again after a few minutes, he says, "Now you know. Stop asking all your questions." Meditation is like that. It is jumping in, not asking questions, not theorizing. It is not investigating but experiencing. The river is the spirit. The spirit is not a stagnant pool at the centre of our being but a flowing river of consciousness – of "living waters." If it is practical, how do we meditate? We meditate by sitting down.

Sit still. Close your eyes lightly and sit as relaxed as you can. Your posture should be comfortable, alert, your back straight. Closing your eyes lightly you then silently and interiorly begin to repeat one word, a single word. You continue to repeat your word through the time of the meditation, silently, interiorly, sounding this single little sacred word. Listen to it as you say it, gently, peacefully, faithfully, come back to it if you get distracted; keep returning to it. There are no special theories or techniques about learning to meditate. Father John summed it up in three words, "Say your word." That was heroic simplicity, especially for a man of his extraordinary gifts. "Say your word." This little word we call a *mantra*. *Mantra* is a Sanskrit term that refers to a sacred text or phrase; it belongs to the traditions of every religious and spiritual family of humankind. It is within Christianity, and Buddhism; it is within Hinduism, Judaism, and Islam. Its essential simplicity is at the centre of all human experience of prayer, of depth, of spirit. The word that you choose should naturally express your faith. For a Christian it would be a Christian word, for a Buddhist, a Buddhist word. The word that Father John recommended was the ancient Christian prayer word, *Maranatha*. Say it as four long single syllables of equal length, Ma - ra - na - tha. Sit down. Sit still. Close your eyes and silently, interiorly, begin to repeat your word from the beginning to the end. The mantra is the simple key to the infinite stream of peace at the centre of our being.

John Main died at peace, in peace, making peace, and giving peace. He died in an atmosphere and an environment conditioned and indeed created by meditation. He was meditating as he lay on his bed and if he was left completely alone, completely silent and undisturbed, he went beyond pain. Everyone in the community was meditating – his care-givers and his spiritual family. As a result of all this, his dying gave life. The environment a person dies in is of great importance. It is not just a matter of interior design and decor but of spiritual awareness, an atmosphere – that sense, beyond understanding, that only the experience of the Spirit can give.

But most people today die in hospitals and most people hate hospitals. They are total institutions, like prisons or schools. Medical scientists in hospitals take over your freedom of choice. They separate you from your family and friends. They relate you to machines; and their reasons for doing this are excellent reasons. Excellent at the level of the mind or the body. But because they ignore the spirit they can be destructive, ignorant and foolish reasons. It is really a very strange thing, this Congress, thirteen hundred people or so from around the world coming to talk about how to help people to die. It is inconceivable in any other period of human history; and I think it suggests how extreme is the crisis of our world. The depersonalization of humanity that has taken place, the dying of the humanness in our technological culture, is our real crisis.

Last year at about this time there were two other international congresses here. One was a meeting of environmental experts talking about the destruction of the ozone layer; and the other was a meeting of Christian meditation group leaders from around the world. Those two and this Congress seem to me to be involved in the same thing – a work of the spirit in our time. A new sense of global unity, involved in universal concerns. What could be more universal than the ozone layer? What could be more universal than meditation? What could be more universal than death? Our hope lies in this global unity. So I think to care for the dying person also means to care for the life of the whole human race and its survival. It will mean doing what you can do, whatever that is, to make the institution human, certainly to prevent it from dehumanizing. That will mean affirming the spiritual, and firstly recognizing and experiencing it for yourself. You can't assert it but you can affirm it. And today we must affirm it, so we must experience it. That is what we do, naturally, by meditating.

Everything we do, or don't do, has its effects. We are responsible for everything we do or don't do. Meditation has its effects, on the patient, on the family, on the caregiver and on the institutional environment that, in our society, brings them together. In the short meetings, the next three mornings, we will meditate and also look in more detail at how meditation can affect the patient, the family and the care-giver. But now, let us meditate. Let us move from words to silence, from ideas to experience, from the parts to the whole and from the periphery to the centre. Now let us allow the mantra to guide us there. You might like to take just a couple of deep breaths just to refresh yourself. Try to sit as still and as quietly as you can.

Let us be co-responsible for the silence that we will share together. Close your eyes lightly, and then silently and interiorly begin to repeat your mantra. Say it with simplicity, gentleness and faith.

"With this in mind I kneel in prayer to the God from whom every family in heaven and on earth takes its name, that out of the treasures of God's glory you may be granted strength and power through God's spirit in your inner being so that through faith Christ may dwell in your hearts in love. So may you attain to fullness of being, the very fullness of God" (Ephesians 3:14-17, 19).

(Meditation)

Good. Would anyone like to raise any questions, any thoughts or any comments at all?

Q. Could you please tell us what "Maranatha" means in English?

A. Yes, it means, "Come, Lord." It is Aramaic, which is the language that Jesus spoke or one of the languages he spoke. It is in the same language as, for example, the word "Abba" (Father).

Q. How is this different from other forms of meditation, like Transcendental Meditation, or prayer; and how does meditation help us relate to other people?

A. The answer to both questions is "unity." First of all it is important to see what meditation, in the Christian tradition that I described, shares in common with other traditions as well as how it may differ. The unity in meditation is more important for us to reflect on. But what makes meditation different as a spiritual practice is that it is not practised as a technique. There's a world of difference between meditating as a technique and as a discipline. We are technologically conditioned and so we think this is a great technique to discover. We think "we will use this and see what we get out of it, improve our performance, and we can let go of it if it doesn't pay off." But as a discipline we bring a dimension of faith and perseverance to meditation. Perhaps we have to practise for some time before we really understand what that faith means. But this is why it is important that meditation is taught as a spiritual discipline rather than merely as a technique because, to put it crudely, you're more likely to get the best results from it as a spiritual discipline rather than as a technique, simply because you're likely to persevere. With faith as your motive force, there's more reason to persevere.

What makes meditation Christian is your Christian faith. It isn't the technique that makes it Christian, Buddhist or Hindu. It is the faith you bring to it. That's why it's such a marvellous way for each person, whatever their faith, to fulfil their faith journey and personally verify the truths of their faith while at the same time sharing deeply a spiritual experience with people of other faiths. The terrible error is saying, "Well, I believe in my faith, and that means that somebody else's faith must be wrong." Logically, intellectually, that is where we get stuck. Somebody must be right and somebody must be wrong. But at the level of the spirit we experience unity, and unity is what meditation leads us to. This becomes quite a perceptible reality as you meditate in a group. You don't communicate through language or through the body at the time of meditation. But there is a deeper communication at work. I think you find too, and this is of particular interest obviously to people here, that when you have meditated with someone you relate to them quite differently and more easily, from a deeper level of personal unity.

Q. I have a couple of comments. One aspect is that there is a strong religious component to meditation and in finding peace. I have some patients who are at the stage of "hopeless-helpless," which is a term we coined yesterday for people who really don't have any belief, and never did have any religious belief.

A. The person of no faith, or no religious belief, can still know they have a centre of mystery to their being. I think you can't persuade anyone they should meditate; but I think you can convince them that they can meditate, that for them to meditate would be a possible and worthwhile journey to make. Each person has to make that journey by taking the first step. I think it's enormously helpful if they have someone they can meditate with regularly. Perhaps in hospital that can be very regularly. The companionship along the way is a very great help. All you need to begin, the only level of faith necessary, is the faith that you exist. The faith that you are really alive awakens a sense of a centre. Everything has a centre, everything has an identity, a true identity. And if we as human beings have a centre, if we have a true identity, then meditation is the journey to that goal. Many people in our kind of world begin with just about that amount of faith and not much more, but that's enough to begin. Perhaps the spiritual role of the care-giver to the dying is to remind people they are still alive, and that death is only part of the whole mystery of life.

Q. Can I add one more comment? To me, meditating itself, the physical aspects of it, seems to be very similar to relaxation techniques with visual imagery or muscular relaxation. Why not use those techniques for people who actually don't have the faith? Would that be of benefit?

A. It could well be. One would use whatever way one could to make it easier for the person. But I think everyone, if you can present meditation as a non-dogmatic spiritual path, can find a wholeness that is deeper than what we can access in mental or physical ways. If they were turned off by Christian language or the religious faith of the person who was teaching them to meditate, then there would be a problem of a communication-resistance to address. But I think with tact and selflessness we could communicate to anyone, who felt the need for peace, an understanding of wholeness as a universal value. We should be able to be spiritual rather than religious and to express holiness as a being-integrated, at peace with ourselves. You don't need to go into a lot of religious dogma to describe that to people.

I think people, especially in our society and especially in the last stages of life, are acutely aware of the need to be at peace with themselves. If you relate the teaching of meditation to people at the point where they are feeling needy and you relate it as a spiritual rather than a physical or an intellectual path, I think they will respond to it out of their deep need for wholeness and integration and peace. The deeper the awareness of need, the deeper will be their response. The other techniques you mentioned seem to me to be more concerned either with psychological adjustment or intellectual peace, maybe, or with physical needs. Those are obviously very necessary. I'm not saying of course that they would not need other things to do and to be helped with, apart from meditation, to help them at those levels as well. But meditation is a particular discipline that goes directly to the centre of the whole person.

Q. Do you think that meditation is more effective if you pray first? Maybe the meditation is more effective because then you have already tried to orientate toward the objective of your meditation, which is finding the centre of your self.

A. Thank you. I think the preparation for the meditation is important. The kind of preparation you would use should be appropriate to the situation and the people involved. In our community, for example, we meditate four times a day together with visitors and guests, and we prepare for the meditation by singing the Divine Office, chanting the psalms and prayers. That's quite appropriate in a community. But I think in other places, say the weekly meditation groups that meet in people's homes or places of work or schools or hospitals around the world, the kind of preparation before the meditation would be different. For some it might involve some reading of scripture, if there was a common faith. I think music is an excellent universal preparation for meditation. Anything that calms the mind and body and enhances the process of focusing, of unifying your attention – calming the mind from its many concerns and distractions – anything that does that really prepares for meditation.

Q. I was listening to the young man a few minutes ago who was objecting to the religious implications of meditation. But isn't it because people confuse the idea of a spiritual plane and a dogmatic religion? Cannot one say that this joint meditation with another is simply getting you to the stream of life and God?

A. Yes, I certainly agree that a very important distinction is to be made, when you are teaching meditation, between dogmatic belief and spiritual faith. One could say there is a difference between faith and belief. You can have faith in the goodness of the human person, in the transcendent potential of the human; that can be enough to get you on to the level of the spirit with another person. But what's really important is simply seeing whether the other person is ready for, or open to, the experience that meditation will lead them to. If they're not, there isn't much point in arguing or splitting theological hairs about philosophical terms. If one can share the experience of silence, then there's something real to talk about. Then the talking will deepen the relationship, and in that new depth faith can jump from one person to another.

Q. Father Laurence, does meditation or the peace come like a triangle to the human body, from the top down, or from the inside of the centre outwards?

A. Well, I think it comes from the centre outwards. All growth in nature is from the centre outwards. Like the flower, all life comes from the centre of whatever is growing. But I think we become conscious of spiritual growth or peace in all dimensions of our being: body, mind and spirit. And in that sense we are a triangle, a triangle of equal sides. We may become more conscious of this new dimension of our life more through one dimension than another at certain times. But ultimately every part of us is touched when anything comes from the centre.

Q. I find it quite exciting to hear a Catholic monk use a Sanskrit word, "mantra." But the issue here is that we're moving toward the centre of our being. And yet I find confusion in trying to help someone come to terms with death because of the question of who or what is dying. Not this "centre." Unless I myself have answered the question, "Who am I?" how am I going to help another?

A. We use the Sanskrit word *mantra* because it is pretty well universal now. I think it is in the Oxford English Dictionary. In the fourth century a Christian monk named John Cassian from whose school we proceed here called his word or phrase a "formula" in Latin. The mantra leads us to the centre of our being and it answers the question "who am I?" through experience. The answer is the experience of deepening personhood. The answer to the question "who am I?" is only found in the transcendence of our ego-identity in the experience of love. That is the deepest religious understanding of the human person, that we come to the fullness of our being in transcendence. That is where death can be seen as being wholly meaningful. In John Main's talk here six years ago, he described how death is part of life, and if we can accept the dying process, the dying of our egoism, the continual cycle of dying and rising (the paschal mystery for the Christian and perhaps even re-incarnation for the Eastern tradition), then death in life becomes meaningful. Then on the final day, in our second death, our last breath has a hopeful meaning because it represents the final transcendence. Meditation gives us a daily experience of that transcendence, of letting go of ourselves, our ego-identity, dying to that and finding ourselves at a continually higher level of reality.

Keeping death before your eyes: Meditation and the dying person

In these three sessions, the most important time that we spend will be in meditation, in silence together. To point us toward that silence, we will begin with some reflections upon the relevance of meditation to your work with the terminally ill. After the meditation, we will have some time for discussion.

I was saying earlier that what a person is doing and needs to do as they prepare for death is to make peace. It is perhaps the most urgent sense a person has when they hear for the first time that death is an imminent reality: that they have to make peace. They have a certain amount of time left, and that time must be used to the full. In his Rule Saint Benedict said that the monk should keep death constantly before his eyes. By saying that, he didn't mean monks to be miserable and morbid. In keeping death constantly before his eyes, the monk was supposed to live fully with a sense of the urgency and the precious value of time. That is the state into which the person, the patient, is thrust when they know that they are going to die. Death is constantly before their eyes. I would like to reflect this morning with you on the way meditation can have an effect upon a person who is in that situation.

The dying person knows that death is constantly present, constantly looming up. In the next two talks we will also look at the way in which meditation has an effect upon the family and upon the care-giver: upon the whole team or triad in which your work and the work of the palliative care are situated.

When a person knows that they are going to die, really not just theoretically, they become urgent about making peace; this peace becomes something that has an actual three-fold relation. Peace is always a matter of relationship: our relationship with ourselves, our relationship with others and our relationship ultimately with God – with the total reality which gives meaning and purpose to our lives. Meditation is about fulfilling that part of ourselves which is about relation and which is in relationship. It means discovering that we are essentially beings in communion. We are not isolated monads. We are not specks of cosmic dust. We are essentially, in our truest identity, in relationship. We are not ultimately alone. Now, meditation for our culture seems like moving away from relationship. It looks like a withdrawal. We think of the contemplative experience as being about withdrawal into solitude or isolation. This is part of the tragedy of our society and culture, that we have lost the awareness of the contemplative experience as being one that realizes our true identity as beings in relationship.

That identity is there to be experienced when we enter into the depths of our own spirit, and come fully into the present moment. That is what contemplative experience means – nothing about mysticism, special visions or revelations. That is not what we are talking about at all. The contemplative experience is one that every single human being is meant for and is capable of. It is simply to be, here and now, totally: body, mind and spirit. The proof that waits for us is that this contemplative experience creates community. Our small community here is, for us anyway, a proof of that. When people enter into that experience of the present moment together, they discover that they are in relationship at a profound level with each other. That seems to me a very important way for the patient to be able to make peace; to begin, in the last stages of their life, this task of making peace.

Peace is not just peace of mind. It is not just control of pain. Peace is a reality of the whole person and therefore a spiritual reality. It is an energy. It isn't just being calm. It isn't just being protected from worry or anxiety. Peace is something positive. It is the harmonized totality of the human person. Animals are not at peace. The human being alone experiences peace. This energy is an interiority: something that arises from the centre of the human person. We can be in the long-desired situation, the long-awaited environment, and still lack peace. We have to be at peace with ourselves if we are to be peaceful. This interiority is also something that passes understanding; something that the mind, reason and even imagination can't fully grasp or fully explain. It has something of the element of gift about it; something of mystery, something beyond ourselves.

Here are three elements worth reflecting on about the nature of peace, and the patient's search for peace:
- It is an energy, something positive.
- It is an interiority, it involves making a journey to the centre, facing oneself, accepting oneself.
- It is transcendent, it passes our understanding.

In the spiritual tradition, in all spiritual traditions, this peace is seen as already within us. It is, in our tradition, sometimes called "the prayer of the heart." It is the spirit that lives at the centre of our being. It isn't primarily a matter of ceremony or ritual, although externals may express and communicate it. They can help a person to come to that peace. But the peace is not in the ceremony, in the ritual, or in the words. The peace is within us. That is the starting point for meditation. There is something deep within us that we are meant to find, to live and rejoice in, and ultimately to share. Now the way of meditation I described yesterday is a way that realizes this faith-conviction. It isn't necessarily a religious conviction specifically, but it is a basic understanding of the human person. This way of meditation is a way that allows that faith-conviction to become real, not just a consoling idea but a reality. At that moment of conscious mortality in one's life too, it is experience that counts, more than words or ideas or consoling theories. The only thing that counts at this point is experience. The only thing that ever counts in the spiritual journey, really, is experience.

The way of meditation is essentially simple. There are no special theories, complicated techniques, no pre-conditioned dogma that you have to hold or subscribe to. It is essentially simple because it is experiential. It is, in fact, a discipline rather than a technique. We have to begin where we are, with whatever kind of faith we may have. All that you need to do is begin; once you have begun you realize that you are entering into a spiritual discipline and that the purpose of a discipline is to set you free. The essence of meditation in this tradition is the discipline of saying your word. It is entering into a faith-filled silence of mind and of body where we leave words and thoughts behind. We are not thinking about God, we are not thinking about ourselves, we are not thinking about our relationships, we are not thinking about peace. We are not thinking or imagining any of these as ideas. We leave words and thoughts and "God" behind. We sit still.

Stillness of body, as far as that is physically possible, is necessary because as we meditate we come into a wholeness of identity: body and mind united in spirit which is the third – the third dimension that is always needed for wholeness. You sit down; you lie down if necessary. The only basic rule of posture, again if possible, is to keep your back straight. None of these rules about externals are essential; but they are helpful. You close your eyes lightly and then silently, interiorly you begin to recite, to repeat, a single word. That mantra could express your faith, whatever that faith may be, or religious tradition you may come from. The name "Jesus" would also be appropriate for a Christian. The Jew, Buddhist, Muslim or Hindu would choose a word that would be suitable to them from within their own traditions. They also have mantras, sacred words, that would be ideal for repetition during meditation. The important thing is to say the word from the beginning to the end of the meditation; to keep returning to it, silently, gently; focusing on it, allowing it to lead you silently, naturally, to the centre of your being. Thoughts, words and images, problems or feelings: let them come and let them go. You are not trying to block them off. They will naturally come but, as naturally, let them go. Stay with your mantra. The mantra has a calming effect upon the whole person because it links each level of our being to the centre where that peace is to be found.

Many people I know have started to meditate after a profound experience of loss that has made them aware of that centre of their being, of that deeper dimension. Here is a key experience in life: the experience of loss, of detachment, of death, of the many deaths we die. An aspect of the experience is emptiness and that key experience we can either repress, ignore, camouflage or bravely enter. If we enter into it we discover that there is fullness there. There is a real sense in which saying your mantra, entering into meditation, is itself an experience of loss and emptiness. You are not going to find instant fullness. Meditation is an acceptance of that key experience of life, an acceptance of the reality of death, an acceptance of what, in the biblical tradition, is called "poverty," an inner not a material poverty, a "poverty of spirit." I think it is important to make the patient aware that meditation is an acceptance of the reality that includes death, not an escape from it. Poverty is not annihilation; poverty is a detachment. Poverty is a non-possessiveness, a letting go which allows us to take full possession of the gift of life.

It seems to me that in many ways meditation can be possible and suitable for patients, at this crucial moment in their life. They have firstly the time to meditate. Ninety percent of the people I meet who say they can't meditate will say it is because they don't have time. They believe in it, but "I simply haven't got the time." Well, a patient has time. It is also, to a person facing death, so utterly simple. Facing the trauma of death or major illness, the patient quite likely does not want to think any more about it, or perhaps does not even have the energy to think, to focus on this problem any more. The great gift of the mantra is that it is a way of being that is also something to do. It is something real to hold on to that puts you into touch with a spiritual reality deeper than thought; deeper than the constant analysis of our situation. It gives a certain distance from the problem of illness, the distance that allows us to accept and integrate it. It brings us into the present moment. It can be done alone or in a group. It can be done at any time. We recommend generally for people to meditate early morning and early evening. That is suitable for people living a normal lifestyle. When you are out of that normal lifestyle it would still be advisable to keep to regular times of meditation: say morning, maybe midday as well and evening. The gift of the mantra deals directly with the great problem of isolation and loneliness because it puts you in touch with that reality in yourselves which is in communion.

I was trying to imagine how this would fit into real situations, and it seemed to me that the idea of a silent hour in a ward or in a hospital could be extremely valuable: times of silence, not when anyone is obliged to do anything but just where silence and stillness are respected and reverenced by the whole ward or the hospital. We have produced a number of tapes which many people (especially those who would find it physically difficult to read) find very helpful, calming and instructive as they prepare for meditation. The important thing, above all, if you were going to introduce meditation to a patient, is that you yourself would be meditating. The relational aspect, the peace-giving, the making of peace, comes from that communication. And the most valuable thing one can do in trying to communicate meditation to someone is to meditate with them; which is what we will do now.

(Meditation)

Q. Could someone use the word "peace" as a mantra?

A. Yes, it would be a possible word. The only thing I would say is that the word you choose as your mantra is not meant to give you something to think about. It is intended to lead you beyond and deeper than thought. So the word should be full of meaning, but you don't want to be distracted by the meaning of it as you are actually saying it. So, for that reason, it might not be such a good idea to take a word that expresses what it is you feel you need most. Which is why it is helpful to take a word not in your own language but that you know the meaning of, so that, as you say it, it doesn't trigger off thoughts and ideas, associations and feelings.

Q. Is the length of the meditation period important?

A. Yes, you have to give it a fair shot. You can't just take a minute here and a minute there. It's like baking bread, you have to leave it in there a sufficient amount of time for it to rise. Twenty minutes is pretty well the minimum amount of time. It takes us almost that length of time to come down to any level of stillness and peace or mental quiet. Thirty minutes is the ideal time but it may take some people a while to build up to a thirty-minute period twice a day. Many people don't find that difficult at first, but some do. What is important is that you set your time and then stick to it. You need to say, "I'm going to meditate for twenty minutes, or twenty-five minutes, and I'll stay in there for that time." That is why it is a good idea to have an external signal so that you don't have to be looking at your watch. It is also always helpful to meditate with others fairly regularly. You will often find that people who begin to meditate in extreme situations of their life, such as your patients would be, tend to get there pretty quickly. A sense of urgency speeds it up because they want to waste less time.

The general process is that, with practice, the mantra roots itself in your consciousness. You will find then that at other times of the day the word will sound. It puts you into touch with that centre of your being where peace is to be found. It is what the New Testament calls "praying at all times." That doesn't mean "saying prayers" the whole time, but rather being in touch with the Spirit that is constant the whole time. I think a terminally ill person would be very likely to find the mantra becoming rooted more smoothly. And so it would be with them at other times of the day as well, and that would be enormously enriching. But it would always be important to set aside particular and regular times, say twice a day, to allow that process to take place and continue.

Being together in truth: Meditation and the family

Yesterday we looked at the effects of meditation upon the patient and a few practical questions arising from that. This morning I'd like to look at the second part of the therapeutic triad: the role of the family, and the effects of meditation on the family of the dying person.

It is worthwhile just saying a word about what we mean concerning the "effects of meditation." I said that meditation isn't a technique. It is not like a medication that you prescribe and of which you predict certain effects or side effects. It isn't a technique to bring about a certain verifiable or measurable result. It is by its nature a spiritual practice, something that concerns the centre of the human person and therefore the whole of the human person. If you are in touch with the centre of something, you are in touch with all of it. Meditation is essentially a spiritual practice concerned with opening the centre of the human person, and so there are effects. There are effects arising from everything we do or don't do; but the effects of meditation are really to be found in the life of the person who is meditating, rather than in what happens during the meditation itself. That is a very important idea to accept and work with when you are beginning to meditate, and certainly if you are trying to communicate meditation to other people. It is not what happens, or doesn't happen, in the period of meditation itself that is really important, but the effects as they reveal themselves in your life as a whole. Those effects will be obviously directly proportionate to the wholeheartedness, or to the faith, with which you meditate. The fewer demands and expectations we have concerning the effects of meditation, the more naturally its fruits will appear and ripen.

Meditation doesn't solve all your problems, either emotional, physical or psychological. You can't present meditation as a cure-all, as a magic cure. But what meditation does is put you into touch with a health, a wholeness, that we call the spirit at the centre of the human person. When we are in touch with that centre it does of course have a real effect upon all the problems and fears of life. The way it does this is to give a new perspective upon those problems and anxieties, those guilts and fears. This perspective can transform the way we face and deal with the particular kind of problems we meet in the care for the dying, or the accompaniment of the dying.

It seems to me that what the family of the dying person really needs is a new idea of prayer. An idea of prayer that would make sense to them as modern people coming from a pluralistic society, from a society that doesn't have a common faith. An idea of prayer that would also make sense to them in the context of their particular situation at that time, with all their complex concerns for the dying member of their family and for their own future. They may be preparing for the death of that person, and soon they may be grieving for the death once it has occurred. Even the most unreligious of people start thinking about prayer when faced with their death or the dying of someone they love. The first thought arises from a childhood conception of prayer as a way to get what you want. In the face of death we want survival. The new idea of prayer here would be that prayer is more than petition. Prayer is not essentially about asking God or a Higher Power for a miraculous intervention.

I think it would be important for anyone introducing a spiritual dimension into the therapeutic situation to be aware that there has to be a distinction between prayer as petition and prayer as an entry into the reality of the situation: into Reality itself. What we are doing when we meditate is accepting the gift of our own being, and if our being happens to be full of joy and light at that moment we accept that. If our being happens to be facing the trauma of death we accept that. It is the acceptance of our own being, as we are, at this moment in our life's journey. That is what meditation is about. It is not trying to regain control over life, not trying to change God's mind, not trying to change our fate or destiny, not trying to reinstate the threatened ego as managing director of our personality. Meditation leads to an acceptance of the reality of the human situation as it is here and now.

For the members of the family of the dying person this acceptance would inevitably involve an entry into the reality of separation. That they are being separated, that they are losing, that they are being cut off from a whole familiar dimension of someone they love and with whom their lives may be fully involved. Meditation is a natural and wonderful way to accept all of that because meditation itself is an experience of radical detachment. We are detaching from our selves; we are experiencing detachment in meditation from our own habitual self-centredness. That is an even greater death than physical death. To die to our self-centredness, our egoism, is not the achievement of just one meditation or perhaps even of ten years of meditation; it is the result of a whole life-time of maturing and loving. That is what meditation is essentially about: a separation, a liberation from habitual self-centredness.

Anyone who can enter that interior experience will face the reality of physical and emotional separation of death in a quite new, more hopeful and more spiritual way. Experiencing that separation is also to embrace something of the solitude of the human condition. Whenever someone is meditating, they are in solitude. We need to make a very important distinction between solitude and loneliness. When we are in solitude we are accepting the uniqueness of our own being, that there is no one else in the world who is me. There is no getting away from that; there is a fundamental quality of uniqueness in the human condition. But this is quite different from loneliness. In loneliness we try to escape our uniqueness, we submerge our personal identity in uniformity. There is nothing more lonely than a crowd. When we are in the process of death we encounter our uniqueness in its total inescapability. You can't escape the fact that it is you who is going to die, or that the unique person you have loved or lived with is going to die. That is an experience of solitude, and meditation gives an interior dimension to that solitude. It gives an ultimate meaning and so a firm hope to that solitude. It enables you to accept reality without loneliness. When we are in solitude we are truly capable of relationship. Meditation would help the family of the dying person to enter the process of their changing relationship, to find perhaps that depth-level of communion from which even death cannot separate us.

Meditation is about silence. It is a language of silence. What we do when we meditate is discover silence as the medium of communication for those experiences that lie too deep for words. In our kind of society, even for the humane medical and professional care-givers in our society, silence is something we need to recover faith in. We need to re-discover the power of silence, the capacity to bond at a level deeper than words and to communicate at a level deeper than thoughts. Meditation for the family of someone dying, as for the dying person, can offer an enormous relief simply because it does not try to communicate our thoughts and feelings. It trusts in the power of silence. In meditation you are not trying to explain what is happening. You are not using ideas, even the most consoling ideas, to explain or to deal with the situation. You have a respite from the effort of words and of the necessity to explain. There are naturally other times for the work of trying to explain, but in meditation there is a necessary relief from that effort. The effort to keep up the chatter, the effort to find the right words, even to have the right kind of concerned expression can create the odour of insincerity or of forcing a response in the attempt to make the correct response.

Meditation gives all involved the resources of silence as a way of being together in truth. If meditation could be gently made available, and taught appropriately in those care-giving situations, it should not be made available as another technique on the program, but as a gift, a spiritual gift ready to be shared when appropriate and when needed. Then those relatives of the dying person could both meditate alone at home when away from the patient and also meditate with him or her in the hospital. That would help establish the communion, the continuous presence that relieves the anxiety of absence and the fears of non-communication.

There is a mysterious truth that I can share with you from my own experience as a monk and as a member of a community. It is that you can feel inseparably close to the people that you meditate with and whose lives you are part of whether you are physically together or not. Union with others at the spiritual level addresses the question of separation that everyone encounters in facing death. What happens is that the reality of the person is awakened on the spiritual level of consciousness. Meditation opens a new sense, a new dimension of the human person, the spiritual at the centre. In meditation you face all the feelings of the human condition; it lifts all the repressed feelings. It is by no means an escape. It is total acceptance. It would make sense to say therefore that to meditate through a time of great anxiety could prevent major experiences being repressed and giving trouble later on in your life. By preventing the major experience or response to that experience being repressed, meditation would enable you to deal with it here and now.

All of these "effects of meditation" depend upon the experience. The experience cannot be forced; it cannot in a sense even be taught. It can only be presented. If the person in the care-giving situation is able to make that experience of silence available to the family, then they have a way of creating a bond and discovering a mutual presence at a deep level of the human person. This in turn enables everyone involved to accept the reality of their situation.

We will meditate now for about twenty minutes. Let me remind you again of the simplicity of meditation. Try to sit as still as you can. Close your eyes and then silently, interiorly, begin to repeat, to recite, a single word. Do not move your lips or tongue as you say it. The word I would recommend is the word *Maranatha*. If you choose that word, say it as four syllables of equal length. In any case, say your word as continually, faithfully and as gently as you can, from the beginning through to the end.

(Meditation)

Q. Does the meaning of the mantra matter?

A. Yes. The word *Maranatha* is Aramaic, a Middle Eastern language, still living, that Jesus would have spoken. Saint Paul ends the first letter to the Corinthians with it, and keeps it in that language even though he writes in Greek. It was clearly a sacred word for the early Christians and its meaning, "Come, Lord," expresses the Christian's faith. The mantra you choose is important because it should express the faith you hold. Meditation is really universal. A Christian can teach a non-Christian to meditate, and a non-Christian can teach a Christian to meditate. The mantra should have meaning to you from your faith. But you then let go of the meaning at least intellectually as you say it. When you meditate you are not thinking about the meaning of the word.

Q. What tools of concentration would help the sick to meditate?

A. How could one help the concentration of those affected by pain? Well, two things I think. One is a teaching on meditation that helps the person to focus. That is the main purpose of the tapes we produce, which are used by meditating groups around the world. They are not meant to stimulate thought before the meditation period but rather to focus concentration as a preparation for meditation; to calm the mind and to centre consciousness. Secondly, I think meditation with others, even one or two others, helps to simplify and concentrate the mind as well. Of course, there are many useful techniques and exercises for relaxation as well as, for example, medication for pain-control. But I think that if you can communicate the simplicity of meditation, and then reinforce it by meditating together, the mantra itself becomes the primary tool of concentration. It would be important to say "do the best you can," and try to give yourself, and anyone you are teaching, the reassurance not to be disappointed by any sense of failure. In faith there is neither success nor failure.

Q. How can meditation be fitted into a busy schedule, and what about the meditation group itself?

A. The time you give to meditation is the best investment of time, even for the next busy meeting. You will find that your next meeting might even be shorter as a result of the time you spent in meditation. I know a large religious order who now begin their council meetings with meditation, and they find it makes everything more efficient. People are less aggressive and more ready to listen. So there is a practical value in meditation for the organization of your time, and that is what modern people are increasingly concerned with – organizing their time.

In leading your meditation group it is important to have an external signal for the meditation period so that you can forget about your watch, and let go of the time fixation that normally preoccupies us in every thing we do. Another good way, which would also help in regard to the earlier question about concentration, and that many people now use, is to make an audiotape with a couple of minutes of quiet music at the beginning and then a blank tape for the period of meditation, concluding with a couple of minutes of more music. That is a gentle way of leading into the meditation and of coming out of it. You don't have to become too concerned about preparing the atmosphere for the meditation. Practice helps to integrate the meditation as something quite ordinary into daily life. In a meditating community, people usually eat immediately after every meditation. They go straight from the meditation room into the dining room. The more naturally you can integrate it into your life, the more fruitful it will be.

Q. Some people come to meditation naturally, without being taught it.

A. Yes, that is perfectly true. In teaching meditation you can make it sound as if the mantra is something that has just been discovered. But I think it is a very natural conclusion to certain states of consciousness that people enter naturally: that we do restrict our consciousness to one word and that one word leads on to full silence. I have met many people who are saying a mantra, are meditating without ever having necessarily been aware of it as something special or different. It's a natural conclusion to a certain journey.

Q. Should the times of meditation be related to meal times?

A. Yes, generally speaking, it's better to eat after meditation and ideally to leave at least a couple of hours after the main meal before meditating.

Q. Is the way of breathing important?

A. Yes. The first aim of meditation is to say the mantra continually, and that is what we have to learn to do. We should breathe naturally. The basic rule is to keep breathing – as naturally as possible. Don't concentrate on your breathing. Give all the attention to the mantra. You will find that quite naturally the mantra will integrate itself with your breathing. Sometimes it coordinates with some other bodily rhythm like the pulse or heartbeat; but most people say the mantra to their breathing. A simple way might be to say the mantra as you breathe in. On your in-breath, breathe it in, and then breathe out in silence. If you find that too long, you could share the syllables of the mantra between the in and the out-breath, and say the first two syllables "Ma-ra" as you breathe in and "na-tha" as you breathe out. But perhaps the simplest way would be to breathe in the mantra and breathe out in silence.

It is very advisable, also, to meditate twice a day. The universal times of prayer are at sunrise and sunset. You will almost certainly find that the second meditation of the day is very difficult to get in. Follow your own experience; but I would urge you not to forget the second meditation because it completes the process. In fact they balance the day in a wonderful way: on these two pillars, as it were, of silence and interiority. When these two pillars support the day's activity, a bridge forms for the work of the day to be connected to the centre of being. To be able to begin and end the day with the experience of silence and stillness is well worth the discipline and effort necessary to make the time available for meditation.

Q. Are meditation groups really useful?

A. Yes, and there are groups pretty well everywhere. They form and develop in a very natural and spontaneous kind of way. They are spreading quite widely. But if you don't find one where you are living, after you have been meditating for a while, you will probably find it quite natural to think of starting one yourself. What you could do is to write to one of our meditation centres where we try to keep up with the groups that are forming; we have some lists to put people in touch with other meditators. We will also be happy to give any advice or help that we can about starting a group if you are interested in doing that. There is a booklet we publish giving simple advice on starting a meditation group which brings together some practical experiences of people who have done this. We suggest a format which begins with a tape, continues into a meditation period and then ends with a discussion. It is a very simple, three-part format that is helped by the resources of books and tapes.

Companions toward death: Meditation and the care-giver

During this congress we have been witnessing one of the signs of the times. I mentioned earlier that there is evidently a global, planetary, unity of consciousness taking place today and expressed through many different movements and organizations. The concerns that this congress represents suggest one expression of that increasingly conscious globalization of humanity. I think some new forms of human interaction will emerge from this form of caregiving. In the book of Genesis, the opening book of the bible, there is the first description of someone who companions people to life – the midwife. Maybe a new form of service, a new type of person, is going to be called for in our society, somebody who companions people to death. This may be particularly needed because death like so many other basic human experiences is now situated in or through institutions. It is vital, for the survival of the human values of those experiences, that institutions remain humanly aware and centred upon the whole person, taking into account the spiritual dimension.

If these new types of service are to be capable of humanizing our institutions, say our hospitals, they have consciously to avoid de-humanization. Therefore the care-giver, whom I'd like to talk about now in relation to meditation, has to be in touch with his or her own centre of wholeness, of the spirit. The care-giver experiences particular problems in relation to their work of accompanying the dying in the last weeks of life. Rather like the family member, they will experience not only the death of the person they are accompanying but also something of their own death. We die with those who die.

If we are genuinely involved, we see the person we are caring for as more than just a job, more than just a patient, a number or a statistic. More than something we are involved in as part of our career, part of our own self-fulfilment. If we see that person as a unique human being, as unique as we are, then we act as if they are really equal to us even though we happen to be healthy at this moment and they happen to be sick and dependent. We can then see them in their dignity, which means in their wholeness, and something of us is going into them and something of them is coming into us. As they die, they are going to die in us and involve us in their death, and we will be intimately affected by their death. The challenge is to maintain the right kind of balance between detachment and involvement. The pressures of professional life, particularly in a humanly intensive profession like the medical profession, create the danger that all the emphasis goes into detachment, professionalism, objectivity and not getting too involved. Yet if that side of the equation is over-balanced, over-emphasized, then we fail to do our job because we fail to be what we are humanly meant to be for that person.

The challenge is how to help without trying to take control. Particularly if you are professionally trained, if you have been to a congress like this, you have heard and absorbed a great amount of insights and statistics and the value of others' experience. You can almost predict the stages that a dying person is going to go through, you can predict your own responses, you recognize patterns. With all that information, the danger is that we become merely users of a skill rather than people who are responding from the centre of our own mystery, from our own wholeness, to the mystery of another person. This seems to me where meditation could be of value to the care-giver in this new kind of role, of accompanying someone to the moment of death, that seems to be emerging in our society. In meditation we relinquish the ego-control factor. That is the emphasis of meditation. As we lift control, we stop trying to manipulate every element of the situation. So our concern becomes less egotistical as we see ourselves less as the centre of the situation, because we can care egotistically. If you happen to be a care-giver you can still be very egotistical in your relationship with the patient. You are giving the care, the other person is receiving it, you are sending it down to them. If the care given is going to be truly efficient from a simple human point of view, it must be efficacious for the wholeness of all the human beings involved. Then clearly we have to operate from a different mind-set, a different attitude than this egotistical, controlling one. Meditation allows that shift of position to happen. It allows for taking off the controls and becoming more receptive, more intuitive and responsive. I would also say it makes us insightful to the real needs of the person. It leads to that necessary combination of commitment and detachment that is involved in all relationship.

Every relationship, if it is a faith-full relationship, whether an intimate one or even a professional one, has to have that balance of detachment and commitment. If one wanted a good definition of faith, one could start from that combination: commitment plus detachment equals faith. Faith here is seen not in terms of religious belief, but in terms of fidelity, faithfulness in a human relationship. Meditation is precisely that experience of faith. As you sit to meditate you are committing yourself to the reality of your own being, your own wholeness. But you are also detaching yourself from any kind of possessiveness or control of yourself or of your reality. It is that combination of commitment and detachment, in relationship to yourself, which then becomes the mode in which you can relate to others. What meditation could help the care-giver to do is to put everything you are into it and then to take everything of yourself out of it: that is what selfless giving is. That is what true service is because that is what pure love is. I don't think one should be frightened, because you are professionals, to say that what you are doing in caring for a dying person is loving them. That doesn't mean you are getting emotional, in a negative sense, over them. It requires of us, I think, a new understanding of love, one that has to be distinguished from our culture and romantic images of love. Love is the energy of the whole person. Love is the power that creates wholeness and bonds the different parts of the human being together.

The care we give has to be love, a love that comes from the centre of our own being and in that sense transcends ourselves. It is never something we are in control of because we can't control our loving another person. Nor is it the same as the professional smile or the professional communication techniques that are perhaps useful and necessary in order to establish the right kind of relationship with those we are caring for. Love is a concern; a compassion that springs naturally, spontaneously, from our own centre, from the depth of our own being – compassion that has that essential human value of conscious naturalness, that comes from the centre. There is always a danger of knowing so much, of observing each patient and each family so objectively, that you look for how well they obey the textbook. Perhaps you have to know your textbook if you are to do a good job but, as Jung said about his work in therapy: know your facts and theories well, but when you touch the mystery of a living person you should forget it all. Forget everything you know. That is what meditation allows us to do because it acquaints us with the practice of letting go of everything we know. When you are meditating you are not acquiring information, you are not developing new skills for control.

The care-giver has to know when to withdraw as well as when to intervene. I think the care-giver therefore has to be a presence; and selfless presence is the key to all successful relationships. It isn't so much a matter of how much time you spend or even what you do with another person, it's rather the quality of your presence to that person. Thirty seconds of real presence can be worth six hours of superficiality or a month of psychological manipulation. It is the presence you bring to those intensely human moments of life or death that is of key value. Presence is also the essence of meditation. Being present. When you meditate, you are simply being yourself, being present. If you meditate with others you enter into another dimension of mutual presence; and as I was saying earlier it is extraordinary, you will discover, how meditation develops and realizes your inter-relatedness with others.

In meditation we enter into the present moment; we leave past and future behind. The way we do that is through the simple recitation of the mantra during the time of the meditation. Sit down, be relaxed, sit still, close your eyes, and silently, interiorly begin to repeat your word, your sacred word, your prayer word, your mantra. Stay with the same word, don't change it. Say it continually from the beginning to the end. It is wholly simple. The basic formula is this: say your mantra until you can no longer say it; and when you realize that you have stopped saying it, start saying it again. That is very challenging because it means we practise a radical detachment. But, if we do it, we are led to the fruit of detachment which is joy, and we are rewarded with the gift of life.

At death's door only one person can go through at a time. But it makes a great difference to know that on this side of the door there is a loving presence to accompany you and to prepare you for the presence that welcomes you on the other side. That seems to me the real mission of the care-giver in this new field: to be that loving presence as fully and as humanly as possible. I hope our times of meditation together have helped you see the great importance of silence and stillness in awakening and communicating this presence.

* * *

Conclusion

At the beginning of our times together, I said I would begin at the end. What I would end by saying is "begin." If you would like to. All you have to do is to want to begin. It is beginning a journey, an adventure, that takes one to the very depths of one's humanity. It is amazing what resources you will find on the way to help you to persevere if you simply begin. Then keep on beginning and never think of yourself, as a meditator, as anything other than a beginner. The only other basic advice is always to keep it simple. We have a tendency to try to complicate things, and meditation is as simple as it sounds. Begin simply and keep it simple. It is very helpful, I think, to feel part of a community because of the communion that meditation naturally creates. If you would like to keep in touch with that community through one of our centres, we would be happy to give any help we can.

Writings of John Main

Word into Silence (London: Darton, Longman and Todd, 1980; New York: Paulist Press, 1981)

Letters from the Heart (New York: Crossroad, 1982)

Moment of Christ (London: Darton, Longman and Todd, 1984; New York: Crossroad, 1984)

The Present Christ (London: Darton, Longman and Todd, 1985; New York: Crossroad, 1985)

The Inner Christ (London: Darton, Longman and Todd, 1987). Combines *Word into Silence, Moment of Christ, The Present Christ*.

The Joy of Being: Daily Readings with John Main (London: Darton, Longman and Todd, 1987)

The Heart of Creation (London: Darton, Longman and Todd, 1988; New York: Crossroad, 1988)

The Way of Unknowing (London: Darton, Longman and Todd, 1989; New York: Crossroad, 1989)

Community of Love (London: Darton, Longman and Todd, 1990)

Writings of Laurence Freeman

The Selfless Self (London: Darton, Longman and Todd, 1988)

Light Within (London: Darton, Longman and Todd, 1988; New York: Crossroad, 1989)

These publications and information regarding the global community of Christian meditation groups and centres may be obtained by writing to one of the following Centres (updated September 1996 by Susan Spence):

International Centre
23 Kensington Square
London W8 5HN
United Kingdom
Tel: 0171 937 4679
Fax: 0171 937 6790

Internet access
WCCM.Archives and WCCM.Forum are available by FTP and WWW at:
ftp://byrd.mu.wvnet.edu/pub/merton/weem/
http://www.marshall.edu/~stepp/vri/merton/WCCM.html

Australia
Christian Meditation Network
P.O. Box 6630
St. Kilda Road
Melbourne, Vic. 3004
Tel: 03 989 4824
Fax: 03 525 4917
Christian Meditation Network
P.O. Box 323
Tuart Hill, WA 6060
Tel/Fax: 9 444 5810

Belgium
Christelijk Meditatie Centrum
Beiaardlaan 1
1850 Grimbergen
Tel: 02 269 5071

Brazil
Nucleo Dom John Main
CP 33266
CEP 22442-970
Rio de Janeiro RJ.
Fax: 21 322 4171

Canada
Meditatio
  P.O. Box 552, Station NDG
  Montreal, Quebec H4A 3P9
  Tel: 514 766 0475
  Fax: 514 937 8178
Centre de Méditation Chrétienne
  Cap-Vic
  367 boulevard Ste-Rose
  Tel: 514 625 0133
John Main Centre
  470 Laurier Avenue, Apt 708
  Ottawa, Ontario K1R 7W9
  Tel: 613 236 9437
  Fax: 613 236 2821
Christian Meditation Centre
  10 Maple Street
  Dartmouth, N.S.
  B2Y 2X3
  Tel: 902 466 6681

India
Christian Meditation Centre
  1/1429 Bilathikulam Road
  Calicut
  673006 Kerala
  Tel: 495 60395

Ireland
Christian Meditation Centre
  4 Eblana Avenue
  Dun Laoghaire, Co. Dublin
  Tel: 01 280 1505
Christian Meditation Centre
  58 Meadow Grove
  Blackrock, Cork
  Tel: 021 357 249

Italy
Centro di Meditazione Cristiana
  Abbazia di San Miniato al Monte
  Via Delle Porte Sante 34
  50125 Firenze
  Tel/Fax: 055 866 7206

New Zealand
Christian Meditation Centre
   P.O. Box 35531
   Auckland 1310
   Tel: 9 478 3438
   Fax: 9 478 6367

Philippines
Christian Meditation Centre
   5/f Chronicle Building Cor.
   Tektite Road
   Meralco Avenue / Pasig
   M. Manila
   Tel: 02 633 3364
   Fax: 02 631 3104

Singapore
Christian Meditation Centre
   9 Mayfield Avenue
   Singapore 438 023
   Tel: 65 348 6790

Thailand
Christian Meditation Centre
   51/1 Sedsiri Road
   Bangkok 10400
   Tel: 271 3295

United Kingdom
Christian Meditation Centre
   29 Campden Hill Road
   London W8 7DX
   Tel/Fax: 0171 912 1371
Christian Meditation Centre
   13 Langdale Road
   Sale, Cheshire M33 4EW
   Tel: 0161 976 2577
Christian Meditation Centre
   Monastery of Christ the King
   Bramley Road
   London N14 4HE
   Tel: 0181 449 6648
   Fax: 0181 449 2338
Christian Meditation Centre
   29 Mansion House Road
   Glasgow
   Scotland G41 3DN
   Tel: 0141 649 4448

United States
John Main Institute
 7315 Brookville Road
 Chevy Chase, MD 20815
 Tel: 301 652 8635

Christian Meditation Centre
 1080 West Irving Park Road
 Roselle, IL 60172
 Tel/Fax: 708 351 2613
Christian Meditation Centre
 322 East 94th Street No. 4B
 New York, NY 10128
 Tel: 212 831 5710
Christian Meditation Centre
 2321 South Figueroa Way
 Los Angeles, CA 90007-2501
Christian Meditation Centre
 2490, 18th Avenue
 Kingsburg, CA 93631
 Tel: 209 897 3711
Hesed Community
 3745 Elston Avenue
 Oakland, CA 94602
 Tel: 415 482 5573
Christian Meditation Centre
 1619 Wight Street
 Wall, NJ 07719
 Tel: 908 681 6238
 Fax: 908 280 5999